GUEST BOOK

FOR

_____

_____

Thank you for coming!

Name

Where have you journeyed from?

Name

Where have you journeyed from?

Name

Where have you journeyed from?

We'd love to hear your thoughts ...

Name

Where have you journeyed from?

Name

Where have you journeyed from?

Name

Where have you journeyed from?

Thank you for coming!

Name

Where have you journeyed from?

Name

Where have you journeyed from?

Name

Where have you journeyed from?

We'd love to hear your thoughts ...

Name
_____

Where have you journeyed from?
_____

Name
_____

Where have you journeyed from?
_____

Name
_____

Where have you journeyed from?
_____

Thank you for coming!

Name

Where have you journeyed from?

Name

Where have you journeyed from?

Name

Where have you journeyed from?

We'd love to hear your thoughts ...

Name

Where have you journeyed from?

Name

Where have you journeyed from?

Name

Where have you journeyed from?

Thank you for coming!

Name

Where have you journeyed from?

Name

Where have you journeyed from?

Name

Where have you journeyed from?

We'd love to hear your thoughts ...

Name

Where have you journeyed from?

Name

Where have you journeyed from?

Name

Where have you journeyed from?

Thank you for coming!

Name

Where have you journeyed from?

Name

Where have you journeyed from?

Name

Where have you journeyed from?

We'd love to hear your thoughts ...

Name
_____

Where have you journeyed from?
_____

Name
_____

Where have you journeyed from?
_____

Name
_____

Where have you journeyed from?
_____

Thank you for coming!

Name

_____

Where have you journeyed from?

_____

Name

_____

Where have you journeyed from?

_____

Name

_____

Where have you journeyed from?

_____

We'd love to hear your thoughts ...

Name
_____

Where have you journeyed from?
_____

Name
_____

Where have you journeyed from?
_____

Name
_____

Where have you journeyed from?
_____

Thank you for coming!

Name

_____

Where have you journeyed from?

_____

Name

_____

Where have you journeyed from?

_____

Name

_____

Where have you journeyed from?

_____

We'd love to hear your thoughts ...

Name

Where have you journeyed from?

Name

Where have you journeyed from?

Name

Where have you journeyed from?

Thank you for coming!

Name

_____

Where have you journeyed from?

_____

Name

_____

Where have you journeyed from?

_____

Name

_____

Where have you journeyed from?

_____

We'd love to hear your thoughts ...

Name
_____

Where have you journeyed from?
_____

_____

_____

_____

Name
_____

Where have you journeyed from?
_____

_____

_____

_____

Name
_____

Where have you journeyed from?
_____

_____

_____

_____

Thank you for coming!

Name

_____

Where have you journeyed from?

_____

Name

_____

Where have you journeyed from?

_____

Name

_____

Where have you journeyed from?

_____

We'd love to hear your thoughts ...

Name

_____

Where have you journeyed from?

_____

Name

_____

Where have you journeyed from?

_____

Name

_____

Where have you journeyed from?

_____

Thank you for coming!

Name

_____

Where have you journeyed from?

_____

Name

_____

Where have you journeyed from?

_____

Name

_____

Where have you journeyed from?

_____

We'd love to hear your thoughts ...

Name

Where have you journeyed from?

Name

Where have you journeyed from?

Name

Where have you journeyed from?

Thank you for coming!

Name

_____

Where have you journeyed from?

_____

Name

_____

Where have you journeyed from?

_____

Name

_____

Where have you journeyed from?

_____

We'd love to hear your thoughts ...

Name

Where have you journeyed from?

Name

Where have you journeyed from?

Name

Where have you journeyed from?

Thank you for coming!

Name

_____

Where have you journeyed from?

_____

Name

_____

Where have you journeyed from?

_____

Name

_____

Where have you journeyed from?

_____

We'd love to hear your thoughts ...

Name

_____

Where have you journeyed from?

_____

_____

Name

_____

Where have you journeyed from?

_____

_____

Name

_____

Where have you journeyed from?

_____

_____

Thank you for coming!

Name

_____

Where have you journeyed from?

_____

Name

_____

Where have you journeyed from?

_____

Name

_____

Where have you journeyed from?

_____

We'd love to hear your thoughts ...

Name

Where have you journeyed from?

Name

Where have you journeyed from?

Name

Where have you journeyed from?

Thank you for coming!

Name

_____

Where have you journeyed from?

_____

Name

_____

Where have you journeyed from?

_____

Name

_____

Where have you journeyed from?

_____

We'd love to hear your thoughts ...

Name
_____

Where have you journeyed from?
_____

Name
_____

Where have you journeyed from?
_____

Name
_____

Where have you journeyed from?
_____

Thank you for coming!

Name

_____

Where have you journeyed from?

_____

Name

_____

Where have you journeyed from?

_____

Name

_____

Where have you journeyed from?

_____

We'd love to hear your thoughts ...

Name

Where have you journeyed from?

Name

Where have you journeyed from?

Name

Where have you journeyed from?

Thank you for coming!

Name

_____

Where have you journeyed from?

_____

Name

_____

Where have you journeyed from?

_____

Name

_____

Where have you journeyed from?

_____

We'd love to hear your thoughts ...

Name

_____

Where have you journeyed from?

_____

Name

_____

Where have you journeyed from?

_____

Name

_____

Where have you journeyed from?

_____

Thank you for coming!

Name

....

Where have you journeyed from?

....

Name

....

Where have you journeyed from?

....

Name

....

Where have you journeyed from?

....

We'd love to hear your thoughts ...

Name

Where have you journeyed from?

Name

Where have you journeyed from?

Name

Where have you journeyed from?

Thank you for coming!

Name

Where have you journeyed from?

Name

Where have you journeyed from?

Name

Where have you journeyed from?

We'd love to hear your thoughts ...

Name
_____

Where have you journeyed from?
_____

Name
_____

Where have you journeyed from?
_____

Name
_____

Where have you journeyed from?
_____

Thank you for coming!

Name

Where have you journeyed from?

Name

Where have you journeyed from?

Name

Where have you journeyed from?

We'd love to hear your thoughts ...

Name

Where have you journeyed from?

Name

Where have you journeyed from?

Name

Where have you journeyed from?

Thank you for coming!

Name

_____

Where have you journeyed from?

_____

Name

_____

Where have you journeyed from?

_____

Name

_____

Where have you journeyed from?

_____

We'd love to hear your thoughts ...

Name
_____

Where have you journeyed from?
_____

Name
_____

Where have you journeyed from?
_____

Name
_____

Where have you journeyed from?
_____

Thank you for coming!

Name

_____   _____

Where have you journeyed from?

_____   _____

_____

Name

_____   _____

Where have you journeyed from?

_____   _____

_____

Name

_____   _____

Where have you journeyed from?

_____   _____

_____

We'd love to hear your thoughts ...

Name

_____

Where have you journeyed from?

_____

Name

_____

Where have you journeyed from?

_____

Name

_____

Where have you journeyed from?

_____

Thank you for coming!

Name

....

Where have you journeyed from?

....

Name

....

Where have you journeyed from?

....

Name

....

Where have you journeyed from?

....

We'd love to hear your thoughts ...

Name

_____

Where have you journeyed from?

_____

Name

_____

Where have you journeyed from?

_____

Name

_____

Where have you journeyed from?

_____

Thank you for coming!

Name

....

Where have you journeyed from?

....

....

Name

....

Where have you journeyed from?

....

....

Name

....

Where have you journeyed from?

....

....

We'd love to hear your thoughts ...

Name

Where have you journeyed from?

Name

Where have you journeyed from?

Name

Where have you journeyed from?

Thank you for coming!

Name

Where have you journeyed from?

Name

Where have you journeyed from?

Name

Where have you journeyed from?

We'd love to hear your thoughts ...

Name

Where have you journeyed from?

Name

Where have you journeyed from?

Name

Where have you journeyed from?

Thank you for coming!

Name

_____

Where have you journeyed from?

_____

Name

_____

Where have you journeyed from?

_____

Name

_____

Where have you journeyed from?

_____

We'd love to hear your thoughts ...

Name
_____

Where have you journeyed from?
_____

_____

_____

Name
_____

Where have you journeyed from?
_____

_____

_____

Name
_____

Where have you journeyed from?
_____

_____

_____

Thank you for coming!

Name

_____

Where have you journeyed from?

_____

Name

_____

Where have you journeyed from?

_____

Name

_____

Where have you journeyed from?

_____

We'd love to hear your thoughts ...

Name

Where have you journeyed from?

Name

Where have you journeyed from?

Name

Where have you journeyed from?

Thank you for coming!

Name

Where have you journeyed from?

Name

Where have you journeyed from?

Name

Where have you journeyed from?

We'd love to hear your thoughts ...

Name

Where have you journeyed from?

Name

Where have you journeyed from?

Name

Where have you journeyed from?

Thank you for coming!

Name

_____

Where have you journeyed from?

_____

Name

_____

Where have you journeyed from?

_____

Name

_____

Where have you journeyed from?

_____

We'd love to hear your thoughts ...

Name

_____

Where have you journeyed from?

_____

Name

_____

Where have you journeyed from?

_____

Name

_____

Where have you journeyed from?

_____

Thank you for coming!

Name

_____

Where have you journeyed from?

_____

Name

_____

Where have you journeyed from?

_____

Name

_____

Where have you journeyed from?

_____

We'd love to hear your thoughts ...

Name
_____

Where have you journeyed from?
_____

Name
_____

Where have you journeyed from?
_____

Name
_____

Where have you journeyed from?
_____

Thank you for coming!

Name

Where have you journeyed from?

Name

Where have you journeyed from?

Name

Where have you journeyed from?

We'd love to hear your thoughts ...

Name

Where have you journeyed from?

Name

Where have you journeyed from?

Name

Where have you journeyed from?

Thank you for coming!

Name

_____

Where have you journeyed from?

_____

Name

_____

Where have you journeyed from?

_____

Name

_____

Where have you journeyed from?

_____

We'd love to hear your thoughts ...

Name

Where have you journeyed from?

Name

Where have you journeyed from?

Name

Where have you journeyed from?

Thank you for coming!

Name

Where have you journeyed from?

Name

Where have you journeyed from?

Name

Where have you journeyed from?

We'd love to hear your thoughts ...

Name

Where have you journeyed from?

Name

Where have you journeyed from?

Name

Where have you journeyed from?

Thank you for coming!

Name

Where have you journeyed from?

Name

Where have you journeyed from?

Name

Where have you journeyed from?

We'd love to hear your thoughts ...

Name

_____

Where have you journeyed from?

_____

Name

_____

Where have you journeyed from?

_____

Name

_____

Where have you journeyed from?

_____

Thank you for coming!

Name

_____

Where have you journeyed from?

_____

Name

_____

Where have you journeyed from?

_____

Name

_____

Where have you journeyed from?

_____

We'd love to hear your thoughts …

Name

Where have you journeyed from?

Name

Where have you journeyed from?

Name

Where have you journeyed from?

Thank you for coming!

Name

_____

Where have you journeyed from?

_____

Name

_____

Where have you journeyed from?

_____

Name

_____

Where have you journeyed from?

_____

We'd love to hear your thoughts ...

Name
_____

Where have you journeyed from?
_____

Name
_____

Where have you journeyed from?
_____

Name
_____

Where have you journeyed from?
_____

Thank you for coming!

Name

....

Where have you journeyed from?

....

Name

....

Where have you journeyed from?

....

Name

....

Where have you journeyed from?

....

We'd love to hear your thoughts ...

Name
_____

Where have you journeyed from?
_____

Name
_____

Where have you journeyed from?
_____

Name
_____

Where have you journeyed from?
_____

Thank you for coming!

Name

_____

Where have you journeyed from?

_____

Name

_____

Where have you journeyed from?

_____

Name

_____

Where have you journeyed from?

_____

We'd love to hear your thoughts ...

Name

Where have you journeyed from?

Name

Where have you journeyed from?

Name

Where have you journeyed from?

Thank you for coming!

Name
_____

Where have you journeyed from?
_____

Name
_____

Where have you journeyed from?
_____

Name
_____

Where have you journeyed from?
_____

We'd love to hear your thoughts ...

Name

_____

Where have you journeyed from?

_____

Name

_____

Where have you journeyed from?

_____

Name

_____

Where have you journeyed from?

_____

Thank you for coming!

Name
_____

Where have you journeyed from?
_____

Name
_____

Where have you journeyed from?
_____

Name
_____

Where have you journeyed from?
_____

We'd love to hear your thoughts ...

Name

_____

Where have you journeyed from?

_____

Name

_____

Where have you journeyed from?

_____

Name

_____

Where have you journeyed from?

_____

Thank you for coming!

Name

_____

Where have you journeyed from?

_____

Name

_____

Where have you journeyed from?

_____

Name

_____

Where have you journeyed from?

_____

We'd love to hear your thoughts ...

Name

Where have you journeyed from?

Name

Where have you journeyed from?

Name

Where have you journeyed from?

Thank you for coming!

Name

_____

Where have you journeyed from?

_____

Name

_____

Where have you journeyed from?

_____

Name

_____

Where have you journeyed from?

_____

We'd love to hear your thoughts ...

Name

_____

Where have you journeyed from?

_____

Name

_____

Where have you journeyed from?

_____

Name

_____

Where have you journeyed from?

_____

Thank you for coming!

Name

_____

Where have you journeyed from?

_____

Name

_____

Where have you journeyed from?

_____

Name

_____

Where have you journeyed from?

_____

We'd love to hear your thoughts ...

Name

_____

Where have you journeyed from?

_____

Name

_____

Where have you journeyed from?

_____

Name

_____

Where have you journeyed from?

_____

Thank you for coming!

Name

_____

Where have you journeyed from?

_____

Name

_____

Where have you journeyed from?

_____

Name

_____

Where have you journeyed from?

_____

We'd love to hear your thoughts ...

Name

_____

Where have you journeyed from?

_____

Name

_____

Where have you journeyed from?

_____

Name

_____

Where have you journeyed from?

_____

Thank you for coming!

Name

_____

Where have you journeyed from?

_____

Name

_____

Where have you journeyed from?

_____

Name

_____

Where have you journeyed from?

_____

We'd love to hear your thoughts ...

Name
_____

Where have you journeyed from?
_____

Name
_____

Where have you journeyed from?
_____

Name
_____

Where have you journeyed from?
_____

Thank you for coming!

Name
_____

Where have you journeyed from?
_____

Name
_____

Where have you journeyed from?
_____

Name
_____

Where have you journeyed from?
_____

We'd love to hear your thoughts ...

Name

Where have you journeyed from?

Name

Where have you journeyed from?

Name

Where have you journeyed from?

Thank you for coming!

Name

_____

Where have you journeyed from?

_____

Name

_____

Where have you journeyed from?

_____

Name

_____

Where have you journeyed from?

_____

We'd love to hear your thoughts ...

Name
_____

Where have you journeyed from?
_____

Name
_____

Where have you journeyed from?
_____

Name
_____

Where have you journeyed from?
_____

Thank you for coming!

Name

_____

Where have you journeyed from?

_____

Name

_____

Where have you journeyed from?

_____

Name

_____

Where have you journeyed from?

_____

We'd love to hear your thoughts ...

Name
_____

Where have you journeyed from?
_____

Name
_____

Where have you journeyed from?
_____

Name
_____

Where have you journeyed from?
_____

Thank you for coming!

Name

_____

Where have you journeyed from?

_____

Name

_____

Where have you journeyed from?

_____

Name

_____

Where have you journeyed from?

_____

We'd love to hear your thoughts ...

Name

Where have you journeyed from?

Name

Where have you journeyed from?

Name

Where have you journeyed from?

Thank you for coming!

Name
_____

Where have you journeyed from?
_____

Name
_____

Where have you journeyed from?
_____

Name
_____

Where have you journeyed from?
_____

We'd love to hear your thoughts ...

Name

Where have you journeyed from?

Name

Where have you journeyed from?

Name

Where have you journeyed from?

Thank you for coming!

Name

_____

Where have you journeyed from?

_____

Name

_____

Where have you journeyed from?

_____

Name

_____

Where have you journeyed from?

_____

We'd love to hear your thoughts ...

Name

Where have you journeyed from?

Name

Where have you journeyed from?

Name

Where have you journeyed from?

Thank you for coming!

Name

_____

Where have you journeyed from?

_____

Name

_____

Where have you journeyed from?

_____

Name

_____

Where have you journeyed from?

_____

We'd love to hear your thoughts ...

Name

Where have you journeyed from?

Name

Where have you journeyed from?

Name

Where have you journeyed from?

Thank you for coming!

Name

_____

Where have you journeyed from?

_____

Name

_____

Where have you journeyed from?

_____

Name

_____

Where have you journeyed from?

_____

We'd love to hear your thoughts ...

Name

_____

Where have you journeyed from?

_____

Name

_____

Where have you journeyed from?

_____

Name

_____

Where have you journeyed from?

_____

Thank you for coming!

Name
_____

Where have you journeyed from?
_____

Name
_____

Where have you journeyed from?
_____

Name
_____

Where have you journeyed from?
_____

We'd love to hear your thoughts ...

Name
_____

Where have you journeyed from?
_____

Name
_____

Where have you journeyed from?
_____

Name
_____

Where have you journeyed from?
_____

Thank you for coming!

Name

_____

Where have you journeyed from?

_____

Name

_____

Where have you journeyed from?

_____

Name

_____

Where have you journeyed from?

_____

We'd love to hear your thoughts ...

Name

Where have you journeyed from?

Name

Where have you journeyed from?

Name

Where have you journeyed from?

41326770R00063